In Defense of the Macedonian Identity

The Best Quotes Proving that Tito Didn't Invent the Macedonians

The League of Macedonian Americans
LOMA

(This page intentionally left blank.)

Published in the United States of America

ISBN: 978-1981378951

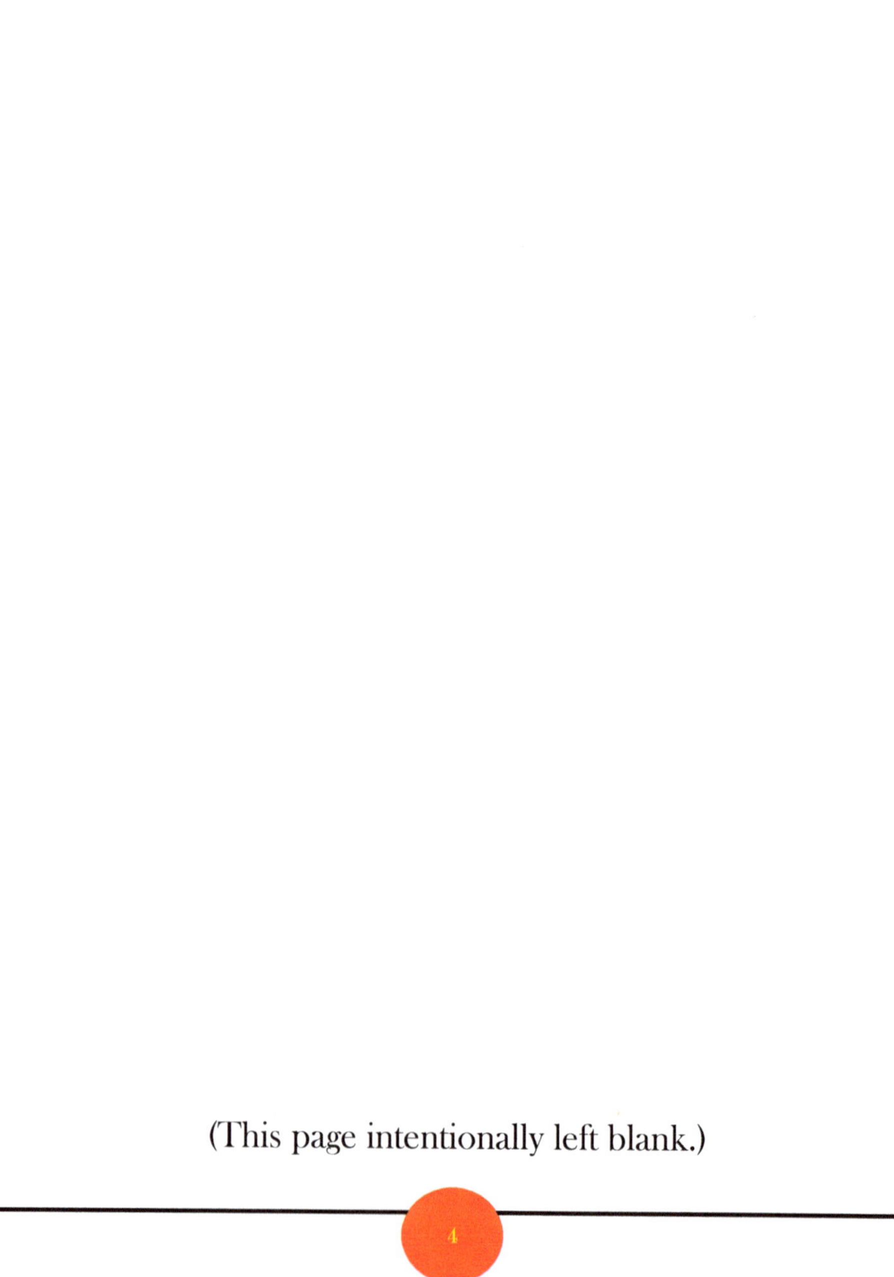

(This page intentionally left blank.)

Introduction

The following compilation of quotes is meant to be a weapon against Greek, Bulgarian, Serbian and Albanian propaganda. Such propaganda often claims that Macedonians do not constitute a separate ethnic group, or that the Macedonian people, their language and culture should not be called *Macedonian*, or that today's Republic of Macedonia has no right to be called *Macedonia*, or that parts of Macedonia should not belong to the Republic of Macedonia. The most common falsehood promoted by Macedonia's neighboring chauvinists is that former Yugoslavian Communist President, Josip Broz Tito, invented the ethnic Macedonians in 1945.

We Macedonians know that such statements are wholly untrue. The Macedonian identity is as old as - or older than - other Balkan peoples' identities. That different peoples have settled, ruled and occupied Macedonia throughout the centuries does not mean that we do not have the right to call ourselves Macedonians. A variety of peoples have settled and occupied Greece, Albania, Bulgaria and Serbia as well; yet, no one is questioning their right to identify as they do. Our ancestors called themselves Macedonians and we have every right to also identify as such.

The reality of the situation is that, for several centuries, Balkan countries have struggled for control of Macedonia. Governments and churches instituted propaganda campaigns that advanced their interests in Macedonia. But when the Macedonians rose up and demanded to be treated fairly and respected as equals, the Balkan countries fell into a frenzy: this tiny nation of Macedonians who they had claimed as their own for many years wanted nothing to do with them. We Macedonians were sick of the wars and struggles over our land and minds; we declared that we only wanted a 'Macedonia for the Macedonians' and that we were separate from and equal to all other Balkan ethnic groups.

Unfortunately, attempts to eliminate the Macedonian identity and nation have only become more exacerbated in recent years. Greece is forcing Macedonia to change its name and won't recognize a Macedonian minority within its borders; extremist Albanian factions have designs on western Macedonia; the Serbian Orthodox Church won't recognize the independence of the Macedonian Orthodox Church; and Bulgaria refuses to accept that Macedonians and the Macedonian language are anything but Bulgarian.

In the old days, such attacks on our people would be met with a violent response. Today, our best defenses are the force of argument and a massive Macedonian reawakening. We Macedonians need to organize around the common Macedonian Cause and arm ourselves with knowledge and a deep understanding of Macedonian affairs. An apathetic and ill-prepared population of Macedonians will only result in our painful demise. We must educate ourselves and unite in a common struggle.

This book by the League of Macedonian Americans (LOMA) is a beginner's guide to the wealth of information that exists on the Macedonian identity and Macedonian Cause **before** Tito came to power in the mid-1940s. While it is only a compilation of quotes, it also provides the readers with sources and resources to further read and understand. Additionally, in these words of Macedonian heroes and foreign observers, we can find the strength and courage to defend our Macedonian name and honor; with this publication, we have another weapon in our arsenal against Balkan propaganda.

LOMA hopes that you find these quotes useful for better understanding the Macedonian situation and motivating you to continue fighting for the Macedonian Cause. Simply memorizing one quote per day will arm you with essential defenses against chauvinistic and discriminatory attacks by uninformed propagandists. While we may never convince stubborn and hateful people to share our views, we can at least fight back.

Long live Macedonia and the Macedonian people!

Their ballads of revolt, in which the word 'Macedonia' recurs in every chorus, prove that they already have a fatherland.

-H.N. Brailsford, Macedonia; Its Races and Their Future, 1906, Pg. 122

I asked him if he was a Bulgarian? 'I'm not.' I asked him if he was a Serb, Greek, or perhaps even a Tsintsar. 'No, I am not. I am a Macedonian from Veles.'

-Mihailo Markovic, Moje Uspomene, 1906, Pg. 316

We have many times heard from the Macedonists that they are not Bulgarians but Macedonians, descendants of the Ancient Macedonians.

-Petko Slaveykov, 1871

The three vilayets or provinces - a term which is still officially applied to the reform area...happens to correspond with the limits assigned by travelers and geographers to Macedonia. There have been, and there still may be living, persons who deny the existence of a country to which that name might be rightly applied. But these ancient names have an unpleasant habit of outliving the work of the gerrymanderers.

-H.F.N. Lynch, Europe in Macedonia, 1908, Pg. 33

Why are we Macedonians a separate nation? The answer to this question is, more than all others, of great political significance. It is well known how Bulgarian as well as Serbian and Greek imperialism deny the existence of the Macedonian nation. According to the first of these, the Macedonians are the 'best part of the Bulgarian nation'. According to the second, the Macedonians are 'pure Serbs', and according to the third, the Macedonians are 'Slavicized Greeks'. Thus, each of our enslavers 'justifies' keeping its respective enslaved part of our enslaved fatherland under its yoke, and at the same time justifies its pretensions for controlling all of Macedonia.

-Bistriski, Fourth Congress of the Macedonian National Association of America, Detroit, Michigan, 1934

Here is what one might say to those who claim that Macedonian as a nationality has never existed: it may not have existed in the past, but it exists today and will exist in the future.

-Krste Misirkov, On Macedonian Matters, 1903

The inhabitants of Macedonia are in the great majority Slavs; they call themselves Macedonians, and what they desire and what we ardently desire for them is an autonomy under European control.

-Sister Augustine Bewicke, January 4, 1919

While my shoulder carries a gun, Macedonia is beyond the reach of the Bulgarian officer.

-Goce Delcev

The Macedonian Slavs considered and called themselves 'Makedonci'.

-R.A. Gallop, 'Conditions in Macedonia', 19 April, 1926

Gloomy and grave, the Macedonian peasant has none of the braggadocio and trifling spirit of the Hellenic peasant. The women, beautiful and chaste, work in the fields like the men...They are a good, strong race, laborious, sedentary, loving their country, and full of promise for their future.

-Saint Paul, Volume 2, 1869, Pg. 111

In the district of Ostrovo/Bitola, nine times out of ten these people, despite being the subject of dispute by three adjoining countries - Serbia, Bulgarian and Greece - would reply in response to the question as to their nationality that they were Macedonians.

-Edmond Bouchie de Belle, La Macedoine et les Macedoniens, Paris, 1922, 80, IV, 303

The Macedonians and the Hellenes, or native Greeks, engage in constant reprisals which sometimes amount to border warfare.

-St. Louis Post-Dispatch, November 27, 1906, Pg. 2

The whole bourgeois press reported yesterday that at the village of Drenova, region of Drama, which is inhabited by Macedonians, an 'anarcho-communist' organization which intended...'to blow up and set fire to the whole town of Drama, was discovered.' ... The workers and the peasants of Greece should protest against the deportations of the Macedonians.

-Rizospastis, April 6, 1934

You, Macedonian, do not listen to them because their words are deceptions. The Balkan monarchies know very well the price of your land. They are not fighting for your wellbeing or for your freedom; instead, they are fighting for the wealth of your land and your enslavement.

-Nikola Pushkarov, 1919

We do not want a Bulgarian Macedonia, but rather a Macedonia for the Macedonians, a Macedonia that is free from tyranny.

-Jane Sandanski, 1904

Neither Greece nor Serbia is expected to give up Macedonian territory for a possible future Macedonia.

-Isaiah Bowman, Constantinople and the Balkans, What Really Happened at Paris, 1921, Pg. 170

The Macedonians were not Greeks.

-Karl Otfried Muller, The History and Antiquities of the Doric Race, Vol. 1, 1830, Pg. xxxiii

The Slavophone population of Serbian Macedonia definitely regard themselves as distinct from the Serbs. If asked their nationality they say that they are Macedonians, and they speak the Macedonian dialect.

-Oliver C. Harvey, 1926

I am a Macedonian Nationalist and I love my mother country intensely. It was only to serve her that I executed this renegade. I am glad I was chosen to sacrifice myself.

-Dimitri Stefanov, January 1925

'What are you reading?' 'Macedonian songs, brother.' He handed me the book -- they were folk songs, written in the Serbian, Macedonian and Bulgarian dialects... 'But listen brother, here there are a lot of Serbian and Bulgarian songs,' I told him. 'They're not Bulgarian nor Serbian. These songs are ours and we are Macedonians -- therefore, Macedonian songs.' Those were the words of my friend Veljko. I wanted to tell him that Macedonians are not a separate people, but in order to not cause a quarrel, I left it alone.

-Hrvatska misao, Volume 3, 1903, Pg. 519

Let them once and for all understand that Bulgarian state nationalism, for which they want to frequently be praised, from 1890 to the present, and Macedonian patriotism are two different things, and not only do they have nothing in common, but they are in direct confrontation with one another. Therefore, all the actions of the Bulgarian government, directed against the autonomy of Macedonia and against the self-imposed movement of the Macedonian emigration ... for us, the Macedonians, were and are only old and new sins against unfortunate Macedonia.

-Ilinden Organization, 1924

I am proud to be known as a Greek, but in truth I am not one. I am a Macedonian.

-Constantine Stephanove, San Francisco Chronicle, July 8, 1901, Pg. 2

It happens that Macedonians who come to Bulgaria continue to call themselves Macedonians ... In Bulgaria, whether they are descended from a Macedonian who travelled eastward in 1878, or whether they are quite recent emigrants, they call themselves Macedonians.

-Henry Baerlein, Fortnightly Review, May 1928, Pgs. 624-632

I asked him what language they spoke, and my Greek interpreter carelessly rendered the answer Bulgare. The man himself had said Makedonski. I drew attention to this word and the witness explained that he did not consider the rural dialect used in Macedonia the same as Bulgarian, and refused to call it by that name.

-Allen Upward, The East End of Europe. London, 1908, Pgs. 204-205

In my opinion a Macedonian cannot be called either a Bulgarian or a Serbian, but simply a Macedonian.

-Rudolf A. Reiss, Sur la situation des Macedoniens et des musulmans dans les Nouvelles provinces Grecques, 1918, Pgs. 6-7

The truth is that the dialect of the Macedonian Slav is neither Servian nor Bulgarian, but 'betwixt and between,' as he is himself.

-Mary Durham, The Burden of the Balkans, 1905, Pg. 60

Oh, Macedonians! It is time we realized that the greatest demon Macedonia must battle against is none other than Bulgaria; and this is why we must keep our interests apart from those of Bulgaria. Common sense demands it.

-Krste Misirkov, On Macedonian Matters, 1903

The Macedonians, who have their own separate language and indisputable ethnic originality, do not have the right to be called Macedonians.

-Henri Barbusse, Monde No. 108, June 28, 1930, Pg. 2

Macedonians! Remember the world's winner, the great glory of Macedonia, the great Alexander of Macedon; remember for the brave King Samoil, the Macedonian giant, for the marvelous Marko Kral, the Slavic glory, that Macedonian blood flowed through them; those of heavenly heights watch and bless our initiated work. To show worthy descendants of their descendants: to preserve their glorious names and to amaze the world with our courage, dexterity and self-sacrifice; to cut off from us the shameful yoke that suffocates us for five centuries.

-Anastas Jankov, 1902

Don't fool yourself, Despot, the national spirit in Macedonia has attained such a state that Jesus Christ himself, if he were to descend from heaven, could not convince a Macedonian that he is a Bulgarian or a Serb, except for those Macedonians in whom Bulgarian propaganda has already taken root.

-Temko Popov, May 9, 1888

Macedonians barely freed themselves from the Greeks and what, now we are going to end up as Bulgars?

-Kuzman Shapkarev, 1870

Macedonians fought side-by-side with the Greeks during the long and bitter struggle for Grecian independence. When the Servians revolted, Macedonians swarmed through the mountain passes to render assistance; when the Bulgarian rebellion broke out, Macedonians hurried to stand side-by-side to fight, and, if necessary to die with men of an alien race having nothing in common with themselves but hatred of the Turkish yoke.

-The World's News, October 24, 1903

Macedonia which revolts, which claims to be a unity and asks for autonomy–there are neither Greeks nor Turks.

--H.N. Brailsford, Macedonia; Its Races and Their Future, 1906, Pg. 80

The inhabitants here [Aegean Macedonia] are no more Serb than the Macedonians of Serbia - they speak Macedonian, and they call themselves Macedonians.

-Oliver C. Harvey, 1926

In the part of Macedonia now subject to Greek rule the language of the current ruling authority is barely understood in the country ... When you ask the people what their nationality is they almost always reply 'We are Macedonians!'

-Major Bernar, 1919

Are you a Serb? Are you Bulgarian? Grecian or Albanian? On this series of questions, the Macedonian people, today as yesterday, were giving the same answer - I am Macedonian.

-Emmanuel Duvillard, early 20th century

Those people whom I had met were insistent on calling themselves neither Serbs nor Bulgars, but Macedonians. There seemed to be no love lost for the Bulgarians.

-R.A. Gallop, 'Conditions in Macedonia', 19 April, 1926

'Neither Bulgar nor Serb' said one such old woman, defiantly, when we left the Monastir road at Dobraveni. 'I am Macedonian only and I am sick of war.'

-National Geographic Magazine, 1917

Just because the Slavs of Macedonia call themselves Macedonians, there was no reason why we or you should consent to give them a name which coincides with a piece of territory.

-C.H. Bateman, October 1922

I was born from my father priest Dimitar and mother Vaskresija as the seventh child of twelve children, five males and seven females. The Slavic letter I learnt from my father, Dimitar Macedonian, who is called like that because we are Macedonians, not Greeks, and his father was called Joseph the priest, and his grandfather Stojmen the priest. I took his nickname Macedonian as well, not because of my father and my grandfather, but to know that we are Slavs of Macedonia.

-Gjorgji Makedonski, 1864

I will teach you French, so you can tell the world that you are Macedonians.

-Goce Delcev, 1897

The Committee, or some sections of it, even contemplates the policy of imposing the Macedonian Slav dialect in place of literary Bulgarian as the language of all the Exarchist schools in Macedonia. Grammars are said to have been printed for this purpose. This seems to me to prove the sincerity of the local autonomist patriotism.

-H.N. Brailsford, Macedonia; Its Races and Their Future, 1906, Pg. 124

This can be accomplished only by the Macedonian population itself, which should announce to the world that it is a separate nation, with a separate history, character and customs, and that it has nothing in common with the surrounding small states. Therefore, it follows that no one has any right to lay claim to Macedonia and it belongs to the Macedonians.

-Memorandum of the Secret Macedonian Committee, June 1887

I will drink to a free and autonomous Macedonia, for which the united Balkan nations fought and suffered so much.

-Jane Sandanski, 1912

The Macedonians must prove to their enemies, both in the Balkans and of the Great Powers, that they are no longer a savage race.

-Pamphlet found on detained IMRO rebel, July 7, 1903

Our fatherland Macedonia has her own history about her past, where one can see her might, glory, as well as her political subjugation under the rule of the then mighty Turkish Empire...Today, every Macedonian, when he mentions the name Aleksandar Makedonski, says: We once had King Alexander the Great. With those words he reminds oneself of the brightest period and glory of the Macedonian State. Aleksandar Makedonski stands before every Macedonian as national pride.

-Kosta Shahov, circa 1900

He is picturesque and peaceable, he works hard in his fields, and in a large number of cases speaks 'Macedonski', which the Serbs call Serbian and the Bulgars Bulgarian, and knows no Turkish, and very little Greek.

-Douglas Walshe, With the Serbs in Macedonia, 1920, Pg. 188

Is there indeed a Macedonian national culture and Macedonian national history? Fortunately enough, we can give an affirmative answer: yes, there is a Macedonian culture and Macedonian national history, distinct from those of the Serbs and Bulgarians, even though they have so far not been the object of extensive and impartial study: the Serbs and Bulgarians have one-sidedly and with a strong bias chosen from Macedonian culture what glorifies their own national name, ignoring questions of capital importance only because they do not concern them or contradict the national aspirations of the choosers and their compatriots. Unfortunately, the independent study of Macedonian history is only beginning now, carried out by those same Macedonians who towards the end of the past century started disbelieving Belgrade and Sofia scholars, who had almost unanimously declared that during the Middle Ages the Slavs were a disorganized people, without national consciousness, who were saved from Greek assimilation only thanks to the establishment of the state of the Turan Bulgars, and later of the state of the Nemanja dynasty. We, Macedonians, believe this to be an erroneous idea as a result of which the Bulgarians and Serbs have wrongly understood not only the history of the Macedonians and Macedonia in the Middle Ages, but also the very history of the Serbs and Bulgarians.

-Krste Misirkov, 1924

Being shocked and increasingly concerned, I struck the village mayor when I heard him speak Bulgarian, which he wishes to call Macedonian, and I recommended that in the future he should always and everywhere speak only Greek, and that he should recommend that his villagers do the same.

-Greek Infantry Lieutenant Dim. Kamburas, January 25, 1925

One of the Macedonian's chief grievances is against the Greek Gendarmerie and during our tour we saw many examples of the arrogant and unsatisfactory methods of the Gendarmerie, who commandeer from the peasants whatever food they want.

-Colonel Corfe, 1926

Those are the six main racial elements. But there are other scraps of peoples – the Albanians, for example, and the Macedonians, and tribes of Moslem Bulgars, and some Asiatic elements brought in by the Turks.

-Frank Fox, Bulgaria, 1915

The Slavs call themselves Makedonci as everywhere else standing between the Serbs and the Bulgarians.

-Hermann Wendel, 1920

In the Kastoria kaza, delegations from the villages came to see us and declared that they wanted neither Greek nor Bulgarian teachers and priests; rather they insisted that they be Macedonians. When questioned about their nationality, they replied that they are Macedonians. These declarations, which are far from being isolated, demonstrate that the Christian population of Macedonia is fed-up with the oppression of the various propagandas, and that in them is beginning to awaken a national consciousness different from those being imposed on them from outside.

-M. Petraiev, 1907

But I repeat that the big mass of the population remained Macedonian.

-Rudolf A. Reiss, 1918

The local Macedonians...view us as usurpers, invaders, and exploiters, they are always hostile toward us and work in unity and systematically to drive us out on every issue.

-Jovan Petrovic, Serb from Skopje, May 1938

In a characteristic Turkish town, the shops were kept by Greeks, the industries carried on by Greeks, Macedonians, and Bulgarians.

-Frank Fox, The Balkan Peninsula, 1915

One hundred and twenty Macedonian families live in this village. They are Macedonians and they do not know any other language except Macedonian. However, nobody should envy the fate of anyone who might be heard by the authorities speaking Macedonian. A threat hangs above his head of being expelled to Bulgaria. All the villagers have relatives in Bulgaria who write to them that the same thing is being done to them by the Bulgarian authorities. However, the Macedonians in Bulgaria have their own organization and they are struggling for their freedom.

-Rizospastis (Greek Communist Journal), July 3, 1935

We Macedonians - not Serbs, not Bulgarians but simply Macedonians.

-Makedonski Golos, June 8, 1915

There is no evidence of any large migrations of Greeks into Macedonia or the more distant parts of the Balkans.

-Arthur Bullard, The Sore Spot of Europe, 1920

I am a Macedonian, I have a Macedonian's consciousness, and so I have my own Macedonian view of the past, present, and future of my country.

-Krste Misirkov, 1925

It is predominantly a Slav region not a Greek one. The language of the home, and usually also of the fields, the village street and the market is Macedonian, a Slav language...The place names as given on the map are Greek... but the names which are mostly used...are Slav names....Greek is regarded as almost a foreign language and the Greeks are distrusted as something alien, even if not in the full sense of the word, as foreigners. The obvious fact, almost too obvious to be stated, that the region is Slav by nature and not Greek, cannot be overemphasized.

-Captain P.H. Evans, December 1944, talking about Aegean Macedonia

Let us not allow the splits and splintering to frighten us. It is, indeed, a pity, but what can we do, since we are Macedonians and suffer from one common disease. If this disease had not been present in our ancestors, from whom we inherited it, they would have never fallen under the scepter of the Turkish Sultan.

-Goce Delcev, May 1899

Language difficulties never daunt a British Tommy, not even modern Greek or Macedonski.

-Douglas Walshe, With the Serbs in Macedonia, 1920, Pg. 188

We have heard other arguments as well. Certain Macedonians consider themselves as separate from the Bulgarians for another reason, for the reason that they are pure Slavs and that the Bulgarians are Tatars.

-Petko Slaveykov, The Macedonian Question, January 18, 1871

Very soon a man emerged from a pile of branches and came near us. He looked nervous and confused and hesitated in his speech. 'Please,' I said, 'Tell us, are you Christian bandits of Turks?' 'Oh,' he said 'We are a mixture of faiths and nationalities. Among us are Bulgarians and Albanians, Serbs and Macedonians. We even have a Jew with us. But we are no bandits. You shall know very soon why you were captured.'

-Katerina Tsilka, 1901

The average Macedonian is neither Serb, nor Greek, nor Bulgar.

-A Foreign Consul in Skopje, 1915, in My Balkan Log, by J. Abraham, 1922, Pgs. 137, 138

It is a grievous error to suppose that we seek to acquire Macedonia on behalf of Bulgaria. We Macedonians consider ourselves to be an entirely separate national element, and we are not in the least disposed to allow our country to be seized by Bulgaria, Servia, or Greece. We will, in fact, oppose any such incorporation with all our might. Macedonia must belong to the Macedonians.

-Boris Sarafov, The Times, London, April 12, 1901

This winter a Macedonian theater group, under the direction of Crnodrimski, gave guest performances in Belgrade and certain other cities of the Kingdom of Serbia. It presented original Macedonian dramas in the Macedonian language. In one word, we had attempts at a new spiritual-cultural literature and art - Macedonian. Let us not fool ourselves. What Crnodrimski presented was not jargon but a tryout of a foreign culture in another milieu.

-Andra Gavrilovic, Brankovo Kolo X 17, 1904, Pg. 516

Sometimes around Goce [Delcev] we felt like one, socialists, anarchists and nationalists, because we thought and acted only as Macedonians, everyone next to another and everyone as one.

-Dimo Hadzhi Dimov

Macedonia will be independent and the Macedonians will remain Macedonians...What the Macedonians want is autonomy for their country, with the intervention of Europe in their favor. No division, no annexation to another state; Macedonia is unique and to the Macedonians. Who can oppose the creation of an autonomous Macedonia? ... Greeks have large claims, it is clear, but after the war of 1897 that they caused, they verified their military incompetence. Macedonians should be recognized and they should be helped to create their own autonomous state in the Balkans, safe and civilized. These people are talented people who would do great deeds.

-Routier Gatson, La Macedoine et la question macedonienne, 1903

A nation is called a people who are of one kind and who speak the same language and who live and associate with one another and who have the same customs and songs and celebrations – these people are called a nation, and the place in which they live is called the fatherland of that nation. So too the Macedonians are a nation, and this place of theirs is Macedonia.

-Georgi Pulevski, Dictionary of Three Languages, 1875

Macedonian patriotism is not artificial; it is natural, a spontaneous and deep-rooted feeling which begins in childhood.

-Captain P.H. Evans, 1944

I was born a Macedonian ... It was written by God for my country to suffer from the Greeks, so they do not give us peace even today.

-Dimitar, Kriva Palanka, 1848

It is true that a Macedonian rarely speaks of himself as a Serb, and this has misled even M. de Laveleye into speaking of all Macedonians as Bulgarians.

-James G. Minchin, The Growth of Freedom in the Balkan Peninsula, 1886, Pg. 95

Macedonians were by no means Greek. They were neither by race, nor by manners, nor by tendencies. Their government was not Hellenic. Their history was analogous to that of the Illyrian, Thracian, and Paeonian peoples, who lived near them, but not to that of the Hellenic cities.

-Arthur de Gobineau, Histoire des Perses, 1869

There are still those of today's inhabitants of Macedonia that do not consider themselves as Serbs or Bulgarians, but a separate ethnicity, probably descendants of the ancient Macedonians.

-Slishkovikj Jakov, Albania and Macedonia, 1904, Pg. 160

Whenever anyone utters a Macedonian word he is punished with 10-15 days in jail. We are called 'ignoramuses' and are constantly beaten. Disciplinary measures are taken every day and we are often ordered to do forced labor. Despite all this we shall continue to speak our language and to sing our revolutionary songs.

-Rizospastis (Greek Communist Journal), August 12, 1934

These Macedonians have a character and a dialect of their own, such as would justify their being considered one of the many distinct Yugo-Slav types.

-Georgy Young, Nationalism and War in the Near East, 1915, Pg. 89

These hostile Churches were the cause of the recent disturbances in Macedonia. Greeks and Bulgarians especially converted the villages with fire and sword, and in Macedonia and all along the Albanian frontier it must never be forgotten, in dealing with the boundary question, that Greek, Bulgarian and Servian means the adherence of the Orthodox Church in those countries, and not necessarily men of those nationalities.

-Wadham Peacock, Albania: The Foundling State of Europe, 1914, Pg. 211

Yet in Southern Macedonia there was at first no enmity between the purely Greek villages and those speaking the Macedonian dialect.

-George Demetrios, When I Was Boy in Greece, 1908

The Turk hates the Bulgar, the Serb hates the Austrian, the Roumanian hates the Greek, the Albanian hates the Montenegrin, the Bosnian hates the Turk, while the Macedonian hates everybody all around.

-William Le Queux, The Near East, 1907, Pg. 20

Do not say the Greeks and the Bulgarians; say the Macedonians.

-H.F.N. Lynch, Europe in Macedonia, 1908, Pg. 13

Therefore, in regard to the question whether the Macedonian dialects are Serbian or Bulgarian, I would answer that they are not entirely either Serbian or Bulgarian, but that most of them belong to an individual dialect type (which may be called the Macedonian language).

-Mieczyslaw Malecki, On the Problems of Macedonian Dialectology, Rocznik Slawistycczny

And the facts say that a great part of the Macedonian population has more a Macedonian than a Macedo-Bulgarian consciousness. According to reliable facts, supplied by our competent comrades of Macedonia itself, the Macedonian consciousness has penetrated quite deeply, especially among the younger generation, which was not exposed to Exarchistic propaganda. According to these comrades, who are fully acquainted with the situation, not less than 80% of the Slavic population in Macedonia considers itself as a Macedonian, and not a Bulgarian population.

-Trajco Kostov, Secretary of the Central Committee of the Bulgarian Worker's Party, 1941

In the elementary schools, the young children who speak their own language are beaten every day. Particularly here in Voden, the henchman and fascist Georgiadis beats the children if they speak their Macedonian tongue, if they wrap their notebooks in red paper, or if they use red ink or red colors.

-Rizospastis (Greek Communist Journal), June 6, 1934

May the residents of Skopje forgive us, along with those who speak a similar language: since they also do not understand our [Bulgarian] language, nor can they speak it.

-Bolgarski, Carigradski Vesnik, October 6, 1851, Pg. 19.

We have already repeatedly declared that this is a question not of nationality, but of humanity. In its solution the Macedonians, who are fighting with an utter disregard for death, are alone entitled to speak, and to no other voice should Europe lend her ear, if she really means to regard the matter as a question of humanity.

-Boris Sarafov, March 14, 1903

The 24th, being the feast of the Macedonian Saints Cyril and Method, is one of the great holidays of the year, when school feasts, 'kerinesses,' &c., take place amid general rejoicing.

-F. Elliot, May 26. 1903

I am not a Bulgarian, but a Macedonian and I wish for Macedonia to have freedom and self-government. This is the goal of all true Macedonians ... We Macedonians are able to raise an uprising in Macedonia to reassure the Great Powers that have signed the Berlin Treaty that they should fulfill what they have promised to Christians in European Turkey, but we are not alone ... We must especially hurry to do this before Serbia and Bulgaria agree on Macedonia. This agreement, in my opinion, would be fatal for the Macedonians, because Bulgaria and Serbia, after they settle for our homeland, will divide Macedonia and those parts will join their own states.

-Anastas Jankov, Stampa, December 1, 1903

Macedonia, as a completely geographical and ethnographic unit, which is fully located in the Ottoman Empire, and occupies approximately the same area as the territories of the free Balkan countries - Greece, Serbia and Bulgaria - with its two convenient ports on the Aegean Sea, has the right to exist and can exist as an independent political entity.

-Hristo Shaldev, 1908

United Front of the Workers and Peasants declares that the struggle for support of the oppressed nationalities: the Macedonians, Turks and Armenians is a general task of all the working population in Greece. This struggle should be directed against spiritual, political and economic oppression and against the forcible Hellenization practiced in schools.

-Rizospastis, August 1932

We the Macedonians do not suffer as much by the Turks ... as by the Greeks, the Bulgarians and the Serbs, who have set upon us like vultures upon a carcass in this tortured land and want to split it up.

-Priest Gologanov, June 22, 1881

There are Bulgarian politicians who are no more our friends than are the Greeks. Under the names of well-known chiefs, they try to send bands into Macedonia to agitate for the annexation idea. What more natural than that we should order them out when they appear? And if they, feeling secure in being of our own flesh and blood, defy us, what can we do but drive them out?

-Member of Dame Gruev's Rebel Band, An Underground Republic, Blackwoods Magazine, 1906

Alexandroff also stated that, if only his demands were granted, the Macedonians would lay down their arms and recognize the Serbian Kingdom, subject, of course, to it being reconstructed as a Federal State in which Macedonia would enter on equal rights with the other members of the Yugoslav Federation.

-Dudley Heathcote, My Wanderings in the Balkans,1925

'You are certainly a Serb?' I asked one of the litigants in court. 'Well, that's how it is now. When the Bulgarians were here I was a 'Bulgarian'. The Serbs arrived, I am now 'Serb', but I am a Christian. 'You want to be closer to the Greeks.' 'No, Greek is something else, I'm a Macedonian.'

-Aleksandar Andrijevic, Strumica: Land and People, 1923

Finally, there is one more phenomenon that cannot be ignored. This is the aspiration of the Macedonians to remain by themselves, which they are trying to attain...And this striving began to be aroused, especially as a result of the contrasts between the Bulgarian and the Macedonian tongues, and between the Bulgarian and the Macedonian characters, since the time when Bulgarian political action began too rashly and sharply to attack the Macedonian features in the name of Pan-Bulgarianism.

-Stojan Novakovic, Bulgarian Schools in Macedonia, Otadzbina XIX, 1888, Pgs. 78-79

Important as the activities of the Macedonian Committee have been and may again be in Bulgaria, they have never gone so far as to compromise the genuine Macedonian character of the movement. It had its origin not in Sofia, but in the little country town of Resna. It is led not by Bulgarians but by Macedonians.

-H.N. Brailsford, Macedonia; Its Races and Their Future, 1906, Pg. 120

The Christians, a herd of Greeks, Bulgarians and Macedonians, with the most villainous faces, morals and manners imaginable, have to be ruled with a tight hand in order to be kept from strangling one another.

-San Francisco Call, July 21, 1890

Macedonians are the oldest Slavs on this Illyrian peninsula, and possibly in Europe.

-Petar Dragasevic, 1871

For long years past the Macedonians have strived for an independent Macedonia, but this was made impossible by the policies of the great powers interested. They were, however, on the verge of achieving this ideal after the First Balkan War, when the interference of Austria in Albania caused Serbia and Greece to demand a revision of the treaty which had provided for Macedonian freedom. Against this demand the Macedonians protested.

-The Story of the Great War, 1919, Pgs. 251, 252

Being neither Turkish nor Greek, we called them Bulgarian, but their language is not Bulgarian, but the Macedonian dialect, and I found lovable people among them, honest, hospitable, and kind.

-George Demetrios, When I Was Boy in Greece, 1908

In English, Slavish and Macedonian languages that fact will be proclaimed throughout Steelton today.

-Harrisburg Telegraph, Tuesday, May 5, 1914, Pg. 7

Through my own studies...I came to the conclusion that Macedonians are a separate nation by its history as well as by its own language.

-Karl Hron, 1899

Thus, the terms Serb, Bulgarian, and Greek have served their time in Macedonia and there is no longer any place for them. It is time for them to be changed for a name common to all Macedonian Slavs, the name Macedonian.

-Krste Misirkov, On Macedonian Matters, 1903

Stand under the flag of autonomy because only under this flag will you fully develop as a nation, and only under that flag will they not beat you because you don't want to be a Greek, Serbian or Bulgarian, but rather you want to remain simply Macedonian.

-Nikola Pushkarov, 1919

Everyone from outside this country who will give us our freedom, will then take our land [Macedonia] from us.

-Petar Poparsov, 1890s

Skopje is located on the border where Dardania ends and Macedonia begins ... and the bridge at the Struma River constitute a border between Macedonians and the Tribalis or Bulgarians.

-Felix Petancic, De itineribus in Turciam libellus, 1522

Here, in Voden, and in our whole district, in the heart of Macedonia, here where we Macedonians do not know any other language but our own Macedonian, various agents of the Greek capitalism force us to speak Greek. Consequently, they threaten us constantly with expulsion to Bulgaria, they call us Komitajis, expropriate our fields, which we have drenched with our sweat just to produce a piece of bread. In addition, they deprive us of the freedom which our fathers won after many years of struggle in which they gave their lives for the liberation of Macedonia. We live under the yoke of Greek capitalism, literally as slaves.

-Rizospastis (Greek Communist Journal), June 6, 1934

It is therefore improbable that the Macedonian question will be revived except through the possible cruelties of Greeks and Serbs in their treatment of the Macedonians.

-Isaiah Bowman, Constantinople and the Balkans, What Really Happened at Paris, 1921, Pg. 170

'They want to force us to become Greeks, in language, in religion, in sentiment, in every way. We have served in the Greek army and we have fought for them: now they insult us by calling us 'damned Bulgars' ... To my question, 'What do you want, an autonomous Macedonia or a Macedonia under Bulgaria?', the answer was generally the same: 'We want good administration. We are Macedonians, not Greeks or Bulgars.'

-Colonel A. Corfe, 1923

Justinian was born at Tauresium, near the modern Skopia, in northwestern Macedonia. His father's name was Istok, and his mother and sister were both called Wigleritza. These names seem to place the Slavonian descent of Justinian beyond a question.

-Edson Clark, The Races of European Turkey, 1878, Pg. 316

Stephen Douchan, ruled victoriously from Belgrade to the Maritza, from the Black Sea to the Adriatic, and assumed the title of 'Emperor of the Roumelians, the Macedonian Christ-loving Czar.'

-James Baker, Turkey, 1879, Pg. 241

We, the undersigned Macedonians, from the bottom of our hearts wish that the complaints of our brothers in northern Epirus may be remedied, since the Macedonians are in the same situation under the bondage of the Greek authorities. We demand the freedom to speak freely in our Macedonian tongue, to open our own schools so that our children will be educated in our own language. We demand that the Greek government should implement the treaties concerning the minorities in regard to the Macedonian minority, which have beet disregarded for so many years. Instead of giving us our rights, the Greek governments are interested only in the 'Hellenization' of our population. On the other hand, with the assistance of their chauvinist newspapers they endeavor to present us Macedonians as 'Slavophone' and 'pure Greeks'. We protest also against the orgies which are being held by various nationalist organizations. Together with the gendarmes, they frequently arrest Macedonians, accuse them of being 'Komitadjis' and subject them to brutal torture. We call upon our brother Macedonians to complain against this situation. Let us demand that an end be put to the terror, let us demand to be given the right for free use of our own language, to open our own Macedonian schools.

-Makedonsko Delo, February 1935, Pg. 8

Macedonia today is again enslaved and divided among the three Balkan states: Serbia, Bulgaria and Greece.

-VMRO May Manifesto, 1924

The civilian population of Salonica is made up largely of Spanish Jews, Macedonians, Gypsies, Greeks, Turks and Dummies (Jews of Mahommedan faith).

-The News Letter: Atlantic Division, American Red Cross, Vol. 11, No. 43, November 10, 1919. Pg. 6

We Macedonians should rise with greater courage and by means of increased activities should reject this campaign because it brings us an even more brutal oppression, starvation, misery and war. Appropriate activities have also been undertaken at the Anti-Fascist Congress. Five hundred drachmas were donated to cover the expenses of our representative. However, this will not do. We should start forming anti-fascist associations, and we should bravely reject the yoke imposed by our oppressors, and create a free and independent Macedonia.

-Rizospastis (Greek Communist Journal), June 8, 1934

But the fact is that Macedonian is not spoken either in Sofia or in Belgrade. It is a separate Slavic language.

-Rudolf A. Reiss, Sur la situation des Macedoniens et des musulmans dans les Nouvelles provinces Grecques, 1918, Pgs. 6-7

Once we reached Macedonia, what struck us most was the ease and zest with which the Macedonian underground battled against the Bulgarian occupying authorities. We stayed there a week and not a night went by without fighting in the streets. It was the same in Bitolj, which the Bulgarian nationalists claim as 'the most Bulgarian of all Macedonian towns.' We found the people there as anti-Bulgarian as they are everywhere in Macedonia. They had organized several groups which at intervals retired into the mountains for training. They were extremely well organized and in contact with all the guerrillas in Yugoslavia, Bulgaria and Greece.

-Michael Padev, Escape From The Balkans, 1944

The insurgent movement is in reality a genuine Macedonian movement, prepared by Macedonians, led by Macedonians, and assisted by the passionate sympathy of the vast majority of the Slav population.

-H.N. Brailsford, Macedonia; Its Races and Their Future, 1906, Pg. 113

A Macedonian Slav is equally intelligible, or unintelligible, to the Servian and to the Bulgarian.

-George F. Abbott, The Tale of a Tour in Macedonia, 1903, Pg. 80

We Are Neither Bulgarians, Nor Greek! We Are Macedonians. Along the northern periphery of capitalist Greece, a whole nation groans under the heavy boot of two-fold, economic and national exploitation and pressure; that is the Macedonian people. The Greek capitalists, landowners and generals, using fire and sword, try to 'Hellenize' these people and make them slaves. However, the long-suffering Macedonian people, who have given so many sacrifices, are not prepared to surrender as slaves to the clutches of their oppressors. They are struggling for their liberation and independence. At their side as their allies stand the Greek workers and peasants who know that 'people who oppress another people cannot be free themselves'. The news report from western Macedonia, which is published below, shows that the Macedonians are waking up and that they are finding the true road towards their liberation.

-Rizospastis (Greek Communist Journal), September 8, 1934

What is most essential for us is internal unity, mutual unity in Macedonia, we do not need Serbs, Bulgarians or Greeks, for we are none of these; we do not need Patriarchists, or Exarchists because we are only Orthodox Christians.

-Krste Misirkov, On Macedonian Matters, 1903

I am not a Bulgarian, I am a Macedonian, a Macedonian Slav.

-Dimitar Blagoev, 1916

We Macedonians have many enemies, and must combat them all, wherever they come from. In the first place the External Committee are our enemies. They are loyal servants of King Ferdinand, and even though they are Macedonians, do not work for Macedonia, but for him.

-Goce Delcev

We should be wary of any direct or indirect attempts by any government to become involved in our affairs as much because of the danger of a bad interpretation from outside as from the point of view of our ideology. We should be deliberately careful and wary in our relations with official Bulgaria because it is a thorn in the side of everyone interested in our problems and struggle and, above all other, she could become for us a wolf which has entered our fold.

-Gjorche Petrov, 1905

It is also important to emphasize that the inhabitants, just as they are not Greeks, are also not Bulgarians or Serbs or Croats. They are Macedonians...The Greeks always call them Bulgars and damn them accordingly...If they were Bulgars, how is it that while they are spread over parts of four countries, one of which is Bulgaria, they consider themselves a single entity and for the most part describe themselves as Macedonians?

-Captain P.H. Evans, 1944

The Macedonian Committee is not an organization of irresponsible adventurers or ex-brigands, but represents the intelligence and patriotism of Young Macedonia. It is led by educated, earnest young men who have fled from Turkish persecution into Greece, Servia, Roumania and Bulgaria to fight for liberty of the fatherland, Macedonia.

-C. Nedelkoff, An Appeal from a Macedonian, Our Day, Vol. 22, No. 9, September 1903

This was the full extent of the proposals he had made so far, though he hoped later on to add a few more, such as that some, at least, of the Judges and administrative officials should be chosen from the Macedonians who had graduated with distinction at a Bulgarian University, and who, although residing within the Principality, were at heart more Macedonian than Bulgarian.

-Sir N. O'Conor, June 5, 1903

Since then Greece and Bulgaria have recognized Macedonian minorities, and Yugo-Slavia has protested that there are no Macedonians. No attempt was made to settle the Balkan States in accordance with race.

-House of Commons Papers, Volume 12, 1929, Pg. 368

Our people were only 'Macedonian Christians,' and then, when Greek propaganda developed they became 'Macedonian Christian Slavs'. It was all the same to us which Christian country would help us to free ourselves from the Turks. I was born in Bitola. There were several grammar-schools in Bitola: Turkish, Greek, Serbian and Bulgarian. It was all the same to us, the Slavs, which Slav grammar-school we attended. For example, alongside many of my friends who later became Bulgarians, I attended the Serbian grammar-school. It is true that the teachers in the grammar-school told us that we were Serbs, just as those in the Bulgarian grammar-school were told that we were Bulgarians; but we kept our own counsel, and that was what our parents told us at home: it does not matter, let them talk, but we are Macedonian Christian Slavs.

-Dimitar Rizov, 1912

Only a strong resistance on our side can save us from other people's upheavals. ... We need to unite, to unite the forces in one power - a people's power, if we want to preserve the future of our homeland. It should be the aspiration of every Macedonian, wherever he may be.

-Loza, 1892

The same thing was true of the hereditary Pashas of Uskup [Skopje] in Northern Macedonia.

-Edson Clark, The Races of European Turkey, 1878, Pg. 170

Bulgarians and Kutsovlachs call themselves Macedonians and the surrounding nations call them Macedonians.

-Vasil Kanchov, Orohidrography of Macedonia, Plovdiv, 1911

In their proclamations the leaders of the Slavo-Macedonian Committee appeal to Alexander the Great as a national hero.

- George F. Abbott, The Tale of a Tour in Macedonia, 1903, Pg. 278

The Greek government has struck us a heavy blow. It has left us at the mercy of Captain Marko Papaterpov, an Andart and goat thief who robs us of our forests which provide a living for 2000 Macedonian families from Dolni and Gorni Nestram. The plundering of the woods have aroused all the villagers, young and old alike. We oppressed Macedonians address you and ask you to help us in our struggle because you have been leading us for some time now.

-Rizospastis (Greek Communist Journal), July 19, 1934

He declares that the insurgents, calling themselves 'Macedonians', demanded a large sum of money from him for his parishioners, and offered to give a receipt, saying the money will be repaid when they came into possession of their country, 'Macedonia'.

-Acting Consul Barker, November 2, 1878

Should the Russians be happy or sad because in Macedonia the indigenous population, who call themselves Macedonians by the old name, are raising their voices? According to our personal opinion it would be just to give at least moral support to this numerous tribe that speaks a separate Slavic dialect and has its own history, not less interesting than the history of the Bulgarians and the Serbs.

-Petar Draganov, 1900

There used to be and there still is an independent Macedonian culture, and it has been the strongest weapon in helping the Macedonians to preserve their present-day cultural matrix and survive all the reversals in the history of their fatherland: not Byzantium nor Bulgaria nor Serbia, nor Turkey, could make changes in the character of the Macedonians of such a nature as to destroy their individuality and estrange them from their Slavic forefathers.

-Krste Misirkov, 1923

The revolutionary traditions of the Macedonian people who, since 1913 have been partitioned among three capitalist states, maintains as a central bright symbol its armed uprising on St. Elijah's Day on August 2, 1903.

-Rizospastis (Greek Communist Journal), August 2, 1934

We young people have therefore been endeavoring for some years past to separate the Macedonian cause from Bulgarian domestic politics. If the rulers of the Principality now declare that they cannot tolerate us as a State within the State, it shows that we have at least succeeded in emancipating ourselves from the pernicious influence of the Bulgarian government. It is only because we are no longer disposed to sacrifice ourselves for this or that party, and regard the liberation of Macedonia as a question of honor for the entire people, that the Bulgarian Government is persecuting us.

-Boris Sarafov, The Macedonian Agitation, 1901

There are over 200,000 Macedonians in Bulgaria, who would return at once to their own country were it under a better government, and they would make Macedonia prosperous and rich.

-Bogirade Tatarchev, Turkish Misrule in Macedonia, The Balkan Question, 1905, Pgs. 173, 174

Are the Macedonians Serbs or Bulgars? The question is constantly asked and dogmatically answered in Belgrade and Sofia. But the lesson of history obviously is that there is no answer at all. They are not Serbs, for their blood can hardly be purely Slavonic. There must be in it some admixture of Bulgarian and other non-Aryan stock (Kuman Tartars, Pechenegs, &c). On the other hand, they can hardly be Bulgarians, for quite clearly the Servian immigrations and conquests must have left much Servian blood in their veins, and the admixture of non-Aryan blood can scarcely be so considerable as it is in Bulgaria. They are probably very much what they were before either a Bulgarian or a Servian Empire existed—a Slav people derived from rather various stocks, who invaded the peninsula at different periods.

-H.N. Brailsford, Macedonia; Its Races and Their Future, 1906, Pg. 101

Whereas, there are wage slaves of Macedonian descent in goodly numbers throughout Canada...Resolved: That the organization of the IWW takes steps as soon as possible to provide literature in the Macedonian language.

-Proceedings of the Second Annual Convention of the Industrial Workers of the World, 1906

We shall struggle for full independence from the Bulgarian, Greek and Serbian whip. We know that we shall be successful - provided we are organized, and provided we enjoy the support of the workers and peasants of Greece. At a conference which we had one of our comrades presented the program and activities of the Internal Macedonian Revolutionary Organization (United). We formed two groups with ten members each, as well as a three-member committee which will organize new groups in all Macedonian villages in the Vrtikop area. We invite all the peasants from the Lerin area and from the area of Enidze Vardar, so that we may start publishing a newspaper for the Macedonians in western Macedonia in our own mother language.

-Rizospastis (Greek Communist Journal), September 8, 1934

There is no place for abstract ideals and sweet dreams in our enslaved country. 'San Stefano Bulgaria' and 'national greatness' -for the Macedonian slave, these are terms that do not warm the soul; and the liberation of Macedonia as a historic national task for Bulgaria is already a dead ideal for him.

-Gjorche Petrov, 1905

We will fight with Greeks because they are our only historic and age-old enemies. Our complete Macedonian national history is full with fights against Greeks.

-Krste Misirkov, 1925

Today, the Macedonians occupy almost the whole coast of the White Sea; in the east they mix with the Bulgarians from Thrace, to the west with the Albanians of Albania and Epirus, and in the north with Serbia in the borderlands of the Shar Mountains. Despite all of this, in their customs and in their language, traces can be found from all those peoples who here and there ruled over them... Macedonians today are characterized independently and stand in the middle among Bulgarians and Serbs.

-Petar Dragasevic, 1871

But even the more educated and moderate Greek, who admits frankly that the Macedonians are Slavs, will add a claim on behalf of Greece to more territory than her sons inhabit, 'in recognition of the civilizing mission of Hellenism.'

-H.N. Brailsford, Macedonia; Its Races and Their Future, 1906, Pg. 201

Macedonia is the common homeland of all those who live here.

-Nikola P. Rusinski, 1901

I have talked a lot with Macedonians in Serbia, in Bulgaria and in the Diaspora, where there is the largest number. Many times I asked them what they are, Serb or Bulgar, where I got a large variety of answers [...] Sometimes I would hear a Macedonian speaking Serbian saying 'I am Bulgarian' and vice versa. That is very funny [...] but also very regretful because most Macedonians are neither Serb nor Bulgar, but just Macedonian.

-Hrvatska misao, Volume 3, 1903, Pg. 517

The same causes which have transferred Armenians into Austria have also brought thither Greeks, Macedonians and Albanians. The people of these different nations indeed are not numerous.

-Charles Green, Austria: Containing a Description of the Manners, Customes, Character and Costumes of the People of that Empire, 1823, Pg. 25

On the other hand, the Macedonians do not think that the rule of the Bulgarian policemen will be much better than that of the Turkish zaptieh, and they will not fight together unless their independence is guaranteed.

-The Literary Digest, Vol. 11, 1895, Pg. 594

Macedonia lay north of Greece. Its people were not Greeks, nor like Greeks in their customs.

-Charles Morris, Historical Tales: Greek, 1908, Pg. 292

But there was one man present who spoke excellent Greek, and who told us that he hailed from a village in the neighborhood named Klabasnitza. It contains 64 houses, not one of them Bulgarian, and the Bulgarians have announced their intention to destroy it. The people speak Macedonian among themselves, but understand Greek as well.

-Allen Upward, The East End of Europe, 1908

It is quite clear that the Macedonian Fascists who keep the Macedonian population of Bulgarian Macedonia under the most cruel of regimes, who have bestially murdered the best Macedonian revolutionaries, who are a tool of the Bulgarian bourgeoisie for the capture of Macedonia and act like bands of murderers against the workers and peasants who fight so heroically against the Fascist dictatorship in Bulgaria; it is clear that they cannot take the lead in the fight for the liberation of the Macedonians and Croatians from the yoke of the pan-Servian military-Fascist dictatorship.

-Balkan Communist Federation, April, 1929

He will appear in his nobleman's costume, will sing in Macedonian and Bulgarian languages, and will also exhibit some Macedonian and Bulgarian curiosities after his address.

-The Scranton Republican, October 31, 1908, Pg. 12

Two groups of Macedonians with nine members each, and another one with six members were formed in the village Eksi-Su. They have assumed the task of enlightening the peasants and organizing the struggle of the Macedonian people for liberation. These groups invite the other villages: Ajtos, Zeleniche and Ljubetino to organize themselves in groups and to make efforts to start publishing a Macedonian newspaper in our own mother language. We should declare in full voice to our Greek masters that we are not Greeks, nor are we Bulgarians or Serbs, but pure Macedonians. We have behind us our history, our past with much fighting for the liberation of Macedonia, and we shall continue our struggle until we finally liberate ourselves.

-Rizospastis (Greek Communist Journal), October 26, 1934

And, what was still worse, a strong party was formed eleven years ago in the three Provinces of Ueskub (Kossovo), Salonica and Monastir, whose members, turning away from the Serbs and Bulgarians by whom they had been abandoned to their fate, inscribed upon their banner the strange device: 'Macedonia for the Macedonians.'

-E.J. Dillon, February 1903

Macedonia, Greece, the south of Italy, Sicily, and north-western Africa, were nearly all that remained to Heraclius of the once vast dominions of Rome.

-Edson Clark, The Races of European Turkey, 1878, Pg. 20

If crime were ever justifiable, ample excuse could be found for Servian committees, Servian bands of brigands and the terrorism of all Macedonian Slavs who refused to confess themselves Servian.

-Herbert Vivian, The Servian Tragedy, 1904, Pg. 278

The Macedonians to the Turke

What just and equal peace can there be betwixt thee and the Macedonians: we desire and endeavor to defend our country, and our laws; thou not content with thine own, thirstest after other kingdoms by force of arms, and seekest to stretch out thine empire beyond thy bounds: we cannot but speak touching our common-wealth, as it becomes our constancie and generous mindes, that we hold nothing dearer, and sweeter among men, than libertie; yet this has always been the common vice and fault among tyrants; free states they hate to death, free cities stand too much in their sight.

-From 'The Turkes Secretoire, Containing his Sundrie Letters', 1607, (undated letter)

The language spoken by the majority of the tillers of Macedonian soil is a Slav dialect, which is not Bulgarian...indeed the Macedonian dialect is no more Bulgarian than the Croatian dialect is Bulgarian, though Bulgarian and Croatian are both unquestionably Slav dialects.

-James G. Minchin, The Growth of Freedom in the Balkan Peninsula, 1886, Pg. 94

The English party, whose interest it is that Greece should become a great and powerful state, with a free constitution, and in which capacity she might be employed as a most powerful weapon against Russian aggrandizement. Should Greece become a great state, of course it will in some degree assist in preventing Russia from getting dominion in the Mediterranean; and should it become a liberal state, with a free press, its papers, spread over its own territory, will communicate with its neighbours, the Macedonians, thence to the Bulgarians, thence to the Wallachians and Moldavians, principalities dependent on and bordering upon the Russian states.

-George Cochrane, Wanderings in Greece, 1837, Pg. 198

The layman was an ardent Macedonian nationalist, rather distrustful of Bulgaria, and profoundly hostile to Russia. The description was good and accurate.

-H.N. Brailsford, Macedonia; Its Races and Their Future, 1906, Pgs. 18-19

Macedonia is one of the European provinces of the Turkish Empire. It is bounded on the south by Epirus, Thessaly and the Mediterranean; to the east by Thrace and the Mediterranean; to the north, by Mount Haemus, Bulgaria and Serbia; to the west, by Albania.

-K.D. Spissarevsky, Macedonia and the Macedonian Question, Pg. 10

Those, too, who have not lived in the East of Europe can scarcely grasp the implicit faith which the peasants of the Greek Church–be they Hellenes, Macedonians, or Montenegrins– place in Russia as the Orthodox Power.

-James G. Minchin, The Growth of Freedom in the Balkan Peninsula, 1886, Pg. 220

Under the third Tsar, Samuel, the eastern provinces were lost, but the Empire remained firmly seated in the west, with its capital at Ochrida, where it maintained its independence till 1018. It was thus definitely a Macedonian state, and Ochrida acquired in the tradition of the Macedonian Slavs a sentimental prestige which it still retains.

-H.N. Brailsford, Macedonia; Its Races and Their Future, 1906, Pg. 96

In Macedonia, the nationality of the Slavs, who form the great majority of the population, has been, especially since 1878, the object of passionate discussions between the Serbs and the Bulgarians who claim each for his race, the totality of these Macedonian Slavs.

-Leon Lamouche, The Balkan Peninsula, 1899, Pg. 21

You can see how these gentlemen treat the issue of autonomy; it would be distasteful to speak of independence for Macedonia in their presence in such circumstances. When the 'liberators' declared war on the Ottomans, not many Macedonians had realized that the destiny of their fatherland had already been decided without their knowledge or consent. Macedonians assumed the war would be fought to liberate and create an independent Macedonian state. It was forbidden to speak and write about Macedonia in Bulgaria, especially about its independence and today's situation is a result of such politics. When Albania became independent and began to establish its statehood, Macedonia was condemned to be divided and destroyed which of course is beginning to happen.

-Jane Sandanski, 1913

Northwards into Macedonia pure Greeks are no longer to be found. All the communities which are included under that designation are Wallachs; or Romounoi, as they call themselves – Greco-Wallachs, as they are called by the Hellenes.

-Valentine Chirol, Twixt Greek and Turk, 1881, Pgs. 37-38

As for the name Bulgarian, which you are giving us, we tell you that we are not Greeks, nor are we Bulgarians or Serbs. We are Macedonians, with our own language, culture, customs, and with our own history. We, who are young, are filled with pride when we listen to our fathers telling us about the Ilinden Uprising, about the heroism of Zlate, Petkov, Gruev, Tosev and Delcev. Were they Bulgarians, Mister Pejo? No, they were Macedonians and they fought for a united Macedonia. All the Macedonians from eastern, central and western Macedonia are uniting, Mister Pejo, in order to kick you out and all the other Greek, Serbian and Bulgarian exploiters.

-Rizospastis (Greek Communist Journal), July 3, 1935

They are fiery eyed men... who live for nothing else than Macedonia, and who, if they thought all hope of freeing it were lost, would scarcely hesitate, like passionate and despairing lovers, to destroy themselves, life having lost for them its sole purpose.

-Paul S. Mowrer, Balkanized Europe, 1921, Pg. 193

Don't expect from me that I feel myself to be a Serb. The Bulgarians have put it into my head for an eternity that I am a Bulgarian. The only thing that I can now say is that I am a Macedonian. Take my children, educate them as Serbs, and they will become Serbs. I have nothing against it. But don't demand any more from us older people.

-Pupil's Father in Macedonia, 1924

Macedonia has its own politics and interests that belong to the Macedonians. He who works for the joining of Macedonia to Greece, Bulgaria, or Serbia, can call himself a good Greek, Bulgarian, or Serb, but not a good Macedonian.

-Goce Delcev, 1900

My place by the sea hospital was now filled up by a physician, a Macedonian, who had studied at Padua: He told me that in the year 1739, the last year of the Turkish War, his countrymen, the Macedonian Christians, had assembled a body of between thirty and forty thousand men, with a design to free themselves from Turkish slavery.

-John Cook, Voyages and Travels Through the Russian Empire, 1770, Pg. 265

It was difficult for a boy to understand the reason of all this hate and bloodshed. I could speak Turkish, and the Macedonian dialect, besides my own Greek tongue, and as a curious boy in the holidays I had been here and there, wishing to know more of the world round me and the people who lived in other villages than mine.

-George Demetrios, When I Was Boy in Greece, 1908

Ferdinand, naturally, desires Macedonia as an extension of his own territory, although the Macedonians are very little in sympathy with his Greater Bulgaria imperialism and would only accept it as an alternative between freedom on the one hand and subjection to Greece and Serbia on the other.

-The Story of the Great War, 1919, Pgs. 251, 252

I am a Macedonian and this is how I see the position of my country: it is not Russia or Austria-Hungary that are the enemies of Macedonia, but Bulgaria, Greece and Serbia. Our country can be saved from ruin only by struggling fiercely against these states.

-Krste P. Misirkov, On Macedonian Matters, 1903

The concept of 'Macedonian Slavic' is confusing only for those who want it to be. Macedonian Slavic is to such an extent a reality that there existed in the nineteenth century a Macedonian literary language, the language of a quite limited scholarly literature but of a voluminous popular literature; and one is not dealing here with documents of folklore such as can be found anywhere: the Macedonian lyric poem, much appreciated in Serbia and in Bulgaria, represents and authentic literary genre, of real value. This literary language, based on dialects which naturally differ among themselves, had not had the time for unification. But its centers were Skopje, Tetovo, Ohrid, Bitola (Manastir), Voden, etc.

-Andre Vaillant, The Problem of the Macedonian Slav, Bulletein of the Linguistic Society of Paris, Vol. 39, 2 (No. 116), 1938, Pg. 195

The legend that Macedonia is a Greek province like Crete and Cyprus, a true limb of Hellas Irredempta, is firmly planted in the European, and especially in the English, mind.

-H.N. Brailsford, Macedonia; Its Races and Their Future, 1906, Pgs. 105

We wonder how many Macedonians -- real Macedonians -- attended the so-called Macedonian meeting recently held in opposition to the cause of Macedonian emancipation in Athens. Possibly one, probably none...But all the distinguished phil-Hellenists in the world, backed by all the pseudo-Macedonians in Greece, cannot get over the fact that Macedonia is in a frightful state of disorder and misgovernment, that there is as much hope of Macedonia being declared Greek as of its being declared Spanish.

-The Pall Mall Budget, January 9, 1885, Pg. 26

If you dare to call yourselves Macedonians, they hunt you down and beat you, you cannot get a job, let alone a pass. You are not allowed to speak the Macedonian language in the institutions and any conversation in Macedonian is noted down as Serbophile. The whole history of the Macedonian people, its culture and struggles, are distorted by the Bulgarian fascists and chauvinists against the will and protests of the Bulgarian working people, in the same way as the chauvinist advocates of a Greater Serbia dealt with the subject until recently, against the wishes and protests of the Serbian working masses and of the highly educated progressive elements among our Serbian brothers.

-Proclamation of the Central Committee of the Bulgarian Communist Party, December 1941

The same tenacity comes out in Macedonian songs, the traditional ones as well as those which have been made expressly in the present war. It is true that the songs usually mention Macedonia and not one particular place in Macedonia, but the feeling, which runs through them, is a simple and direct love of country, not an intellectual enthusiasm for a political ideal...Passing through them all is the Macedonian's love of the place he lives in.

-Captain P.H. Evans, 1944

We are Macedonians, not Greeks or Bulgars. Give us a good father and we will be good children. We don't want bands of any sort coming to our villages. We want to be left in peace.

-Colonel Corfe on the common Macedonian peasant desires in Aegean Macedonia, 1924

'What language do you speak?' I asked the peasant... 'I am a Macedonian,' he replies, 'you know, the Serbs maintain that our language is a Serbian dialect, the Bulgarians say that we speak Bulgarian. What can you do about it?'

-Gerhard Christoph, 1931

The modern Greeks are no more the pure strain of Pericles than the Macedonians are ethnically clear descendants of Phillip of Macedonia.

-Arthur Bullard, The Sore Spot of Europe, 1920

The salvation of the Balkan peoples is in the autonomy of Macedonia. Macedonians want this autonomy because they see it as a solid guarantee for the peace, tranquility and fraternal life of the inhabitants of the Balkans. A shared Macedonia would be the source of countless misfortunes, an autonomous Macedonia would be a hotbed of civilization, the rendezvous of the noble and peaceful emulations in the way of work and intellectual culture. If Macedonia acquires its autonomy, all nationalist hatreds that gnaw it will be extinguished, and the small Balkan states that groan under the weight of their financial crises, can finally emancipate themselves from their harmful rivalries and devote themselves to a beneficial labor for their prosperity. What misfortunes could be spared if the Balkan peoples considered the Macedonian question as it is by the Macedonians themselves.

-Les Reforms, 1901

Because Macedonia is the reason for many troubles between Greece, Bulgaria and Serbia, why wouldn't we create an independent Macedonia? After all, the Macedonians do not recognize any nationality except Macedonian.

-L'Action Francaise, July 29, 1919

Who thinks about Macedonia? We Bulgarians do not talk about Macedonia, but others speak and think about it - they are the Macedonians themselves ... Do not forget that Macedonians really are like the 'Slavic Irish' - in them the national consciousness is strongly developed and so that is how their fighters are born.

-Aleksandar Stamboliyski, Bulgarian Prime Minister, 1922

These Slavs may properly be considered as a special Macedonian group, but since they were closely related to both Bulgars and Serbs and had, moreover, in the past been usually incorporated in either the Bulgar or Serb state, they inevitably became the object of both Bulgar and Serb aspirations and an apple of bitter discord between these rival nationalities. As an oppressed people on an exceedingly primitive level, the Macedonians Slavs had as late as the congress of Berlin exhibited no perceptible national consciousness of their own...in fact, so indeterminate was the situation that under favorable circumstances they might even develop their own Macedonian consciousness.

-Ferdinand Schevill, The History of the Balkan Peninsula, 1922, Pg. 422.

Poor Georgie! He spoke a Slav dialect, and was possibly a mixture of all the races that have ever ruled the peninsula, and all he had gained was a Mauser ball through his right hand in the name of Alexander the Great... A song was sung during the late Macedonian insurrection in which an eagle, who is soaring over the land, asks what is the cause of so much excitement, and is told that the sons of Alexander are rising.

--Mary Durham, The Burden of the Balkans, 1905, Pg. 6

The German tribes passed into Europe to the north of the Black Sea, while another migration, from which sprung the Lydians, Phrygians, Thracians, Macedonians, Greeks, and Romans, settled the western regions of Asia Minor, and passed on into the South of Europe.

-Edson Clark, The Races of European Turkey, 1878, Pg. 315

But the other Macedonian stocks are not peoples of the soil. The Albanians are recent invaders. The Vlachs are nomad herdsmen, wandering carriers and cosmopolitan merchants, whose families are scattered all over the Levant. The Greeks are townsmen, reared on abstractions, who care nothing for the soil of Macedonia, and very much indeed for 'Hellenism.'

-H.N. Brailsford, Macedonia; Its Races and Their Future, 1906, Pg. 122

Macedonians! Today, as before, you have no political or cultural freedom. While the Serbian officials did not allow you to call yourselves Macedonians and persecuted those who disobeyed, now the Bulgarian fascists and chauvinists force you to call yourselves Macedonian Bulgarians, also persecuting those who say they are Macedonians. They represent your leaders and fighters from the past, such as Goce Delcev, Pere Tosev, Gorce Petrov, Jane Sandanski and Dimo H. Dimov, completely as Bulgarian chauvinists and fascists...What a disgusting desecration of the memory of your great apostles! What a filthy distortion and falsification of the Macedonian struggle for freedom!

-Proclamation of the Central Committee of the Bulgarian Communist Party, December 1941

King Marko is the son and pride of Macedonia and one of the three great conquerors who spread the name of their land far beyond its territories: (1) Alexander of Macedon spread the glory of Macedonia as far as the Central Asian rivers of Amu Darya [Oxus] and Syr Darya [Jaxartes], and also to India and the Indian Ocean; (2) The holy Cyril and Methodius spread the Macedonian word and script among all the Slavic peoples, and (3) King Marko placed under his authority and under that of the Macedonian muse all popular singers and peoples on the Balkan Peninsula, including you, the descendants of his sworn enemies.

-Krste Misirkov, 1923

In the central stretches of the Balkans, Macedonia, the people spoke practically the same Slavic dialect, but did not line up sharply with either of the rival nationalities.

-Arthur Bullard, The Sore Spot of Europe, 1920

Who are the Macedonians? Yugoslavia claims they are Serbs; Greeks claim they are Greeks who speak Bulgarian and call them 'Vulgarophones'; Bulgarians hold they are Bulgarians, and most of the Macedonians assert that they are Macedonians.

-Emil Lengyel, 1934

A struggle to control Macedonia set in, which was one of the saddest pages in church history. Serb, Greek, Bulgar, prelates, school teachers, bandits, set out to make Macedonians join their church.

-Arthur Bullard, The Sore Spot of Europe, 1920

But don't you believe for one minute that the revolutionaries are working towards an autonomous Macedonia that would, in the end, be incorporated into Bulgaria. God Forbid! That will never be...All of us Macedonians, no matter where we are, no matter how educated we are, none will allow Macedonia to be incorporated into any other...Instead, we will work towards incorporating other provinces to her. We, the intelligentsia, were educated by the Russians, Romanians, Serbs and Bulgarians...However, none of us will become slaves to any of these and at any cost. Instead, they will immediately go to their own flock, as we too have done...We have a glorious element, and our people is resilient. And once Macedonia gains autonomy, then Bulgaria will sooner become Macedonian rather than Macedonia - Bulgarian. We have a real chance for that to occur...In Bulgaria, the highest positions are held by Macedonians...without question, when the time comes, today's notables, Macedonian by nationality, will come over to us and Bulgaria will be Macedonian...We believe this will be so sooner or later...Macedonia will be a state and she will look towards drawing other states in a union as cantons and, that way, she will be powerful country.

-Kosta Shahov

The Greek takes higher ground. His mind moves among abstractions. He talks not of Greeks, but of Hellenism, not of fact, but of right. That Hellenism has a right to Macedonia is his thesis, and he is never at a loss for an argument. He begins of course with Alexander. It does not trouble him that in classical times the Greeks possessed only a few isolated colonies on the Macedonian coast. He waves aside the objection that for the ancients, Alexander and his Macedonians were no better than barbarians.

-H.N. Brailsford, Macedonia; Its Races and Their Future, 1906, Pg. 194

A section of the Macedonian emigrants has been made use of by the Bulgarian counter-revolutionary movement, to repress the revolt of the Bulgarian workers and peasants. The conduct of the duped Macedonians, who, in the guise of Macedonian revolutionaries, became the mercenaries of the Bulgarian bourgeoisie and the executioners of the Bulgarian working people, is a deliberate attack against the very cause of Macedonian liberation itself. The Macedonian workers must emphatically condemn this attack.

-Balkan Communist Federation, March 1924

The overwhelming majority of the Macedonian people is convinced that its freedom can only be won in mass action in concert with the other victims of oppression and exploitation in Yugoslavia, Greece, and Bulgaria, the three countries which oppress Macedonia, and with the victims of exploitation and oppression all over the world. The masses in Macedonia are therefore rallying more and more round their real organization, United I.M.R.O., which is working for the overthrow of oppression by means of a mass insurrection, for the right of self-determination for the Macedonian people, for the secession of Macedonia, and for the establishment of an independent republic of the working people.

-Dimitar Vlahov, November 1934

If once you take money from the government under current political conditions, that implies engagement and ties...The Bulgarian government harbors the desire to rule Macedonia. As soon as it begins to provide money, it will know how to use the situation which its help will create and will not be content with a platonic relationship, only with tangible benefits. Moreover, other Balkan and European countries already maintain that the Organization is inspired by Sofia ruling circles... All these considerations force us to look for other means, other sources, always independent of Bulgaria.

-Goce Delcev

The Greeks call us 'Slavophone Greeks' and the Serbs 'true Serbs'. Why? So as to justify their rule and their oppressive aspirations toward Macedonia. The Bulgarian chauvinists act in the same way. They exploit the relationship between the Macedonians and the Bulgarians and characterize us as an 'indivisible section of the Bulgarian nation.' The Bulgarian imperialists have always aspired to conquer and enslave Macedonia, not liberate it...We must state it so that all hear, that we are not Serbs, nor Greeks, nor Bulgarians. We are Macedonians, a separate Macedonian nation. Only in this way can we best defend the independence of our movement and our right for an independent Macedonian state.

-VMRO (United), 1935

During the whole 30 years of its existence as a state, Bulgaria has carried out an anti-Macedonian policy. Flattering and attracting the Macedonians to its side, at the same time it persecuted them with ferocity and hatred and strove to destroy in them any idea of an autonomous Macedonia; while doing so, the Bulgarians did not shrink from using any means. Thus, in 1888, the Bulgarian Government destroyed the 'Macedonian Literary Society' under the presidency of Georgi Pulevski ... Two years later, in that same Sofia, the Bulgarian Government closed the evening schools, specially opened for the emigrant Macedonian craftsman, and the heads of those schools, Macedonian patriots - Damjan Gruev, Delchev, Petre Pop Arsov and many others - were expelled from Bulgaria.

-Dimitrija Cupovski, 1913

Our dear Macedonia, our dear homeland is calling: You, who are my faithful children; you, who like Aristotle and Alexander the Great, are my heirs; you, in whose veins Macedonian blood flows, do not leave me to die, help me. What a sad sight, real Macedonians, it would be if you were to witness my burial.

-Macedonian Provisional Government, March 23, 1881

www.ingramcontent.com/pod-product-compliance
Lightning Source LLC
Chambersburg PA
CBHW040226240726
48664CB00001B/31

9781981378951